WHO'S THE GOAT?

USING MATH TO CROWN THE CHAMPION™

TROUT VS HARPER VS BETTS VS RUTH

David Aretha

rosen publishing's rosen central

New York

Published in 2020 by The Rosen Publishing Group, Inc.
29 East 21st Street, New York, NY 10010

First Edition

Library of Congress Cataloging-in-Publication Data

Names: Aretha, David, author.
Title: Trout vs. Harper vs. Betts vs. Ruth / David Aretha.
Description: First edition. | New York : Rosen Publishing, 2020 | Series: Who's the GOAT? Using math to crown the champion | Includes bibliographical references and index. | Audience: Grades 5–8.
Identifiers: LCCN 2019009930| ISBN 9781725348561 (library bound) | ISBN 9781725348554 (pbk.)
Subjects: LCSH: Baseball players—Rating of—United States. | Trout, Mike, 1991– —Juvenile literature. | Harper, Bryce, 1992– —Juvenile literature. | Betts, Mookie, 1992– —Juvenile literature. | Ruth, Babe, 1895–1948—Juvenile literature. | Mathematics—Juvenile literature. | Baseball players—United States—Biography—Juvenile literature.
Classification: LCC GV865.A1 A74 2020 | DDC 796.3570922 [B]—dc23
LC record available at https://lccn.loc.gov/2019009930

Manufactured in the United States of America

CONTENTS

INTRODUCTION

Babe Ruth was famous for—among many other things—eating a lot of hot dogs. One story has him consuming at least a dozen between the games of a doubleheader in April 1926, after which he was hospitalized. Despite his horrible eating habits, the Great Bambino recovered to bat .378 in 1926. A year after that, he set a Major League Baseball (MLB) record with sixty home runs.

Babe Ruth, according to almost all baseball historians and most statistical calculations, is the greatest player of all time—but was he? Was an overweight, late-night partier who chugged beer, smoked cigars, and binged on hot dogs really better than the fitness-freak players of today?

Babe Ruth's waist size was around 40 inches (101.6 centimeters)—determined by wrapping a tape measure around one's belly. Mike Trout, fit and powerful, boasts a waist size of just 33 inches (83.8 cm). Low body fat and lean muscle allows Trout to swing a bat with lightning quickness and run around the bases lickety-split. Fellow modern-day superstar Bryce Harper is equally lean, and 2018 American League (AL) Most Valuable Player (MVP) Mookie Betts is the slimmest of the bunch. All three of these phenoms can sprint from

Major League Baseball is made up of the American League, founded in 1901, and the National League, which dates back to 1876.

home plate to first base in just seconds. Ruth would not have been able to make it anywhere close to the bag in that amount of time.

With that in mind, why is Ruth considered the GOAT—greatest of all time? In short, it is because he dominated his competition more than any other player in history. In 1919, he set the MLB record for homers in a season with twenty-nine. In 1920 for the New York

Yankees, he belted fifty-four. Nobody else in the league had more than nineteen that year.

Moreover, Ruth is the only man in MLB history to star as both a hitter and a pitcher. He won ninety-four games on the mound and lost only forty-six, mostly with the Red Sox in the 1910s. His career earned run average (ERA) was a sterling 2.28.

Trout, Harper, and Betts rank among the brightest stars of modern baseball. All are in their twenties, and each has won a league MVP award. When Trout crushed a pitch one day in 2018, the ball left his bat at 118 miles per hour (mph) (189.9 kilometers per hour). Harper and Betts have also rocketed balls over 110 mph (177 kph). Each player hits for a high batting average, launches a ton of home runs, steals bases, and shines defensively in the outfield.

In the face of updated technology, training, and talent, some have argued that Ruth no longer has sole claim to GOAT status. Using both simple and advanced math calculations, it is possible to help determine who among these stars should actually be considered the greatest. Numbers will show that Ruth reigned supreme in his era—but who is the best player today? More important, can anyone touch the records and legendary feats of the Great Bambino?

All statistics are taken from baseball-reference.com unless otherwise noted.

CHAPTER 1

BABE RUTH, THE GREAT BAMBINO

In his prime, George Herman "Babe" Ruth was unquestionably the biggest star in the biggest sport in the United States. As he strode to the plate at Yankee Stadium—known as the House That Ruth Built—fans rose to their feet. They stood in awe of the larger-than-life slugger, the living legend. With strength straight out of a folk story, the Great Bambino could wallop baseballs 400 to 500 feet (121.9 to 152.4 meters)—even topping 600 feet (182.9 m) one day in Pittsburgh,

The Babe made such an impact that the National Baseball Hall of Fame and Museum features a room dedicated solely to Ruth.

Pennsylvania. "I swing big, with everything I've got," the Babe once said, as recorded on Baseball-Almanac.com. "I hit big or I miss big. I like to live as big as I can."

A SHINING STAR

Born in 1895, Ruth grew up in an apartment above his father's saloon in Baltimore, Maryland. As a child, he ran the streets and rarely attended school. He was eventually sent to St. Mary's Industrial School for Boys, where he lived for much of his childhood and teenage years. It was also there that Brother Matthias, one of the overseers at the school, taught him the game of baseball.

In 1914, Ruth signed with the minor league Baltimore Orioles, where he stunned fans with his majestic home runs and lights-out pitching. On July 4, 1914, the major league Boston Red Sox acquired him. In his first four seasons with Boston, Ruth primarily pitched. From 1915 to 1917, he posted win-loss records of 18–8, 23–12, and 24–13. In 1916, he led the American League with a 1.75 earned run average (ERA).

To calculate ERA, the number of earned runs the pitcher allowed is divided by the number of innings he pitched; this quotient is then multiplied by nine. The ERA is thus the average number of runs a pitcher allows in a nine-inning game. For Ruth in 1916:

$$63 \div 323.67 = .1946$$

.1946 × 9 = 1.75

In 1918, Ruth played more in right field and pitched less. As a result, he led the American League in home runs with eleven. The years 1900 to 1919 were known as the Dead Ball Era in major league baseball. The baseball was softer back then, meaning players could not whack it as far. Ruth, a powerful 6-foot-2 (188 cm) brute who took massive swings, could blast it a great distance and

Ruth first made an impact as a left-handed pitcher with the Boston Red Sox. While posting a league-best 1.75 ERA in 1916, he did not give up a home run all season.

do so more consistently than other players. In 1919, he socked twenty-nine home runs to set the new major league record. After the 1919 season, the Red Sox sold Ruth's talents to the Yankees for $25,000.

THE SULTAN OF SWAT

In 1920, it seemed like nearly everyone in New York was coming out to see the mighty Ruth. Though homerless in April, he belted ten longballs in May and kept on smashing after that. Tales of his heroics spread across the nation—mostly in newspapers, since games were not broadcast on the radio yet. In June in St. Louis, Missouri, three cowboys met Ruth in the Yankees locker room. They had ridden their horses for three days from Wyoming just to see the great Babe Ruth, the "Sultan of Swat."

Ruth finished 1920 with fifty-four homers—shattering the MLB record of twenty-nine—and he did not just whack home runs. His batting average was a dazzling .376. No major league player has batted that high since 1994. Batting average is calculated by dividing a player's total number of hits (singles, doubles, triples, and home runs) by their total number of at-bats:

$$172 \div 458 = .376$$

Also in 1920, the Babe led the American League with 150 walks, 158 runs scored, and 135 runs batted in (RBI). Moreover, his .847 slugging percentage set a major league record that stands to this day.

Slugging percentage (also known as slugging average) is a fairly complicated statistic. It starts with total bases. In the total bases calculation, a single is worth 1 point, a double 2, a triple 3, and a home run 4. In 1920, Ruth had 73 singles, 36 doubles, 9 triples, and 54 homers. So, his total bases can be calculated:

$$(73) + (36 \times 2) + (9 \times 3) + (54 \times 4)$$
$$73 + 72 + 27 + 216 = 388$$

The total bases number is then divided by number of at-bats to figure out the slugging percentage. For Ruth in 1920:

$$388 \div 458 = .847$$

The 1920s were called the Roaring Twenties as wealth in America ballooned and people began moving to big cities and spending more money on cars, fashions, fancy homes, and artwork. Radio, movies, jazz music, and dancing became all the rage during this exciting time. Throughout the decade, Babe Ruth personified this joy, this power, and this over-the-top lifestyle. Ruth belted 467 home runs in the 1920s alone, while batting .355 ($1{,}734 \div 4{,}884 = .355$) during the decade.

The Bambino swung with all his might—and often missed. He set the Major League record for a hitter with 1,330 career strikeouts.

CHANGING THE GAME

The Babe made the home run so popular that Major League Baseball officials changed the game. They ordered new baseballs that would travel farther when hit. This made such a difference that the 1920s and 1930s would become known as the Lively Ball Era, as homer totals surged.

In 1921, Ruth crushed 59 homers, totaled a career-high 168 RBI, and scored 177 runs—more than any MLB player scored in the 1900s or 2000s. In 1927, Babe became the first to launch sixty home runs in one season. No one would break this record until Roger Maris of the Yankees cracked sixty-one in 1961.

Ruth and hulking first baseman Lou Gehrig—batting third and fourth in the lineup for the Yankees—were a powerful duo in the 1920s. Together, they led their team to World Series titles in 1923, 1927, 1928, and 1932. The 1927 Yankees lineup was known as Murderers' Row.

A BOY'S DYING WISH

In 1926, Johnny Sylvester—age eleven—was kicked in the head by a horse. Doctors feared that the New Jersey boy had only a short time left to live. For some reason, during his hospitalization, Babe Ruth was mentioned. Some say that Johnny requested a Babe Ruth–autographed baseball as a dying wish. Others claim that his family thought that such a gift would cheer him up.

Soon, the family sent an urgent telegram to the Yankees requesting a Ruth autograph. The Babe happened to be in St. Louis preparing for game four of the 1926 World Series. Johnny was still very much alive when he received a special airmail package—balls signed by the Yankees and Cardinals players plus a special note from Ruth, as reported in a *New York Times* article by Robert Thomas Jr.: "I'll knock a homer for you on Wednesday."

The Babe belted not just one homer for Johnny on Wednesday, but three. The inspirational story made all the newspapers, and when he returned to New York, Ruth met Johnny in the hospital. Ironically, Ruth died young while Johnny—now part of baseball folklore forever—lived to a ripe old age.

They scored 975 runs in 154 games, an amazing average of 6.3 runs per game ($975 \div 154 = 6.3$). They boasted a 110–44 record. They set an American League record with a winning percentage of .714. Winning percentage is calculated by dividing a team's number of wins by the number of games in which it played:

110 ÷ 154 = .714

In game four of the 1926 World Series, Ruth socked three home runs. In game three of the 1932 World Series, he performed his fabled "called shot." Standing at home plate, he pointed toward the center field seats at Chicago's Wrigley Field—and then immediately smacked the next pitch into those seats.

Whether on the field after the game or at a nearby hospital, Ruth often took time to sign autographs for children.

When Ruth retired at age forty in 1935, he had amassed 714 home runs. Prior to the Babe, Roger Connor had held the MLB record with just 136 dingers—an enormous difference of 578 (714 – 136 = 578). He also set MLB records for career RBI (2,213) and walks (2,062), though both marks have since been broken. His .690 career slugging average, however, remains an MLB record.

Off the field, children loved Babe Ruth, and vice versa. He liked to dress up as Santa Claus and hand out presents, and he spent countless hours signing autographs for kids. After retiring as a player, he deeply desired to manage the Yankees. However, despite his contributions to the game, the team turned him down, believing he was not disciplined enough.

Not long after that, the Bambino's years of hard drinking and smoking caught up with him. He developed throat cancer, and in August 1948, he died at age fifty-three. His body lay in state in the rotunda at Yankee Stadium out of respect for the greatest player the game had yet seen. More than one hundred thousand mourners filed past his casket, saying goodbye to the Babe and thanking him for brightening their lives.

CHAPTER 2

MIKE TROUT, THE MILLVILLE METEOR

On video, many of Mike Trout's home run–saving catches almost look fake. One such example took place on September 26, 2015, in front of nearly forty thousand fans at Angels Stadium. Trout had robbed a bunch of homers in center field before this, but he would have to soar to catch this one. In a close and important game, Seattle's Jesus Montero launched a high flyball destined to clear the fence by several feet. Trout knew he could not jump that high, but he had a plan. He sprinted back to the padded wall and stuck his spike into it, launching himself upward. A millisecond later, he placed his right hand on top of the wall to give himself further lift. Although the ball was high above ground, he stretched out his left arm and had just enough height to catch it.

Climbing a ballpark's wall to save a homer is one of the ultimate defensive baseball fantasies, and Trout truly lived the dream after that catch. Statcast is a high-technology tool used to measure MLB players' skills. It uses cameras, radar, and computers to measure speed and distance. These measurements include the speed of the ball leaving the hitter's bat (exit velocity) and how fast an outfielder runs to catch the ball. On that epic catch, Statcast measured Trout's footspeed to the fence at 17.4 mph (28 kph). He had a route efficiency rating of 97.7 percent. That means he ran a near-perfect route (nearly a straight line) to the ball. Those skills are amazing, but it was his climb and catch that will forever be remembered—and this was just one example in a career full of "wow" moments.

Trout climbs the far wall to make his famous catch against the Seattle Mariners on September 26, 2015.

THE "MILLVILLE METEOR"

The son of former minor league player Jeff Trout, Mike enjoyed an idyllic childhood in a small New Jersey town. He starred in baseball and basketball in school, playing shortstop and wearing the number 2 jersey in

The Los Angeles Angels debuted in the American League in 1961. The team's name has changed many times since then.

honor of his idol, Derek Jeter. Yet he was not consumed by sports. He credited his parents for showing him a path to being humble with his talents, not someone who shows off or has an arrogant attitude. Growing up, he did not even dream of being an MLB superstar.

At Millville Senior High School, Trout began to realize he had big-league potential. He set a New Jersey high school record with seventeen home runs in a season, while scouts gushed about his extraordinary combination of speed and power. The Los Angeles Angels of Anaheim drafted Trout late in the first round in 2009. The "Millville Meteor" rocketed through the minor leagues. He earned Minor League Player of the Year awards in both 2010 and 2011 and played forty games with the big-league Angels late in 2011. He began 2012 in Salt Lake City, but after he smashed a

.402 batting average through twenty games, the Angels promoted him to the majors for good.

As LA's rookie center fielder in 2012, Trout broke enough records to fill a book. Of all his feats, this may be the most impressive: he became the first player in major league history to total 30 home runs, 45 steals, and 125 runs scored. Mike cracked 182 hits in 559 at-bats for a .326 batting average (182 ÷ 559 = .326). He was not only named AL Rookie of the Year, he finished second in AL MVP voting. He even won MLB's Heart & Hustle Award.

ANGELIC WAR-IOR

Incredibly, Trout has compiled similar numbers in most of his professional seasons. From 2012 through 2018, he totaled 235 home runs, 185 steals, and 773 runs. To determine the average number of each per year, divide each statistic by the number of seasons (in this case, seven):

235 ÷ 7 = 34 homers per year
185 ÷ 7 = 26 steals per year
773 ÷ 7 = 110 runs per year

Over that span, as well, he batted an impressive .310 (1,160 ÷ 3,747 = .310). Among current MLB players,

Great athleticism, perfect swing mechanics, a sharp eye, and supreme confidence help make Trout one of the game's top hitters.

Trout owns the highest career slugging average (through 2018) at an incredible .573 (2,219 ÷ 3,870 = .573).

Trout also draws a lot of walks, leading the AL three times with a high of 122. He amasses walks partly because he has a good eye at the plate and also because pitchers are reluctant to give him anything good to hit. From 2016 through 2018, he led the league in on-base percentage (OBP) each season, with a high of .460 in 2018; this meant that he reached base safely in approximately 46 percent of his trips to the plate.

The formula for OBP is somewhat complicated: (hits + walks + hit-by-pitches) ÷ (at-bats + walks + hit-by-pitches + sacrifice flies). In 2018, Trout had 147 hits, 122 walks, 10 hit-by-pitches, 4 sacrifice flies, and 471 at-bats:

(147 + 122 + 10) ÷ (471 + 122 + 10 + 4)
279 ÷ 607 = .460

With his tremendous offensive production and stellar work in center field, Trout was an AL MVP candidate seven times through 2018. He won the award in 2014 and 2016, and finished second four times. Even in 2017, when he played in only 114 of 162 games due to injury, he finished fourth in MVP voting.

His secret to success? Besides his natural talent, Trout brings supreme confidence into the batter's box. Even if a pitcher throws a blistering fastball alongside sharp-breaking sliders and curveballs, Trout believes he is going to win the battle. "You have to just go in that box and own it," he told Tom Verducci of *Sports Illustrated*. "Think positive, and it's yours."

In the 2010s, a statistic called wins above replacement (WAR) has become popular. It is a very complex statistic with many variables. A player with a WAR rating of 5 or better for a season is an outstanding MLB player—most likely playing at the all-star level. According to the calculation, a player with a 5 rating

GPOAT: GREATEST PITCHER OF ALL TIME

Though many fans and experts believe only hitters and position players should be in the running for GOAT consideration, pitching in baseball is equally important. The legendary Cy Young holds the record for most wins with 511, but that does not make him the greatest pitcher in the eyes of most. During Young's career (1890–1911), pitchers often started forty to fifty games in a season and frequently pitched all nine innings. They had a chance to rack up a lot of wins.

Cy Young was a sixteen-time twenty-game winner. He won thirty or more games five times during his career.

Walter Johnson (1907–1927) is the only other pitcher to record at least 400 wins. The following is a list of some of the best starting pitchers ever and their statistics. Note that ERAs can be deceiving; pitchers in the Dead Ball Era had lower ERAs since fewer runs were scored in general. Tons of runs were scored in the 1920s, 1930s, 1990s, and 2000–2009, all eras featuring a lot of offensive dominance.

Pitcher	Years	Wins		Wins + Losses		Winning Percentage	ERA	Strikeouts
Cy Young	1890–1911	511	÷	826	=	.619	2.63	2,803
Christy Mathewson	1900–1916	373	÷	561	=	.665	2.13	2,504
Walter Johnson	1907–1927	417	÷	696	=	.599	2.17	3,509
Lefty Grove	1925–1941	300	÷	441	=	.680	3.06	2,266
Warren Spahn	1942; 1946–1965	363	÷	608	=	.597	3.09	2,493
Sandy Koufax	1955–1966	165	÷	252	=	.655	2.76	2,396
Bob Gibson	1959–1975	251	÷	425	=	.591	2.91	3,117
Nolan Ryan	1966; 1968–1993	324	÷	616	=	.526	3.19	5,714
Tom Seaver	1967–1986	311	÷	516	=	.603	2.86	3,640
Roger Clemens	1984–2007	354	÷	538	=	.658	3.12	4,672
Greg Maddux	1986–2008	355	÷	582	=	.610	3.16	3,371
Randy Johnson	1988–2009	303	÷	469	=	.646	3.29	4,875
Clayton Kershaw	2008–2018	153	÷	222	=	.689	2.39	2,275

With so many talented pitchers taking the field over the years, it is difficult to determine the GOAT—just as it is with hitters. In the end, a table full of statistics is valuable, but nothing compares to watching the greats play and seeing their impact on the game.

is worth five additional wins to his team as compared to a replacement-level player (meaning a player who may be added to the team for minimal cost).

Trout led the AL in WAR four times through 2018, and twice finished second. He twice achieved a WAR rating of 10.5 in a season. This meant he was worth approximately 10.5 wins to the Angels—all by himself. He is considered baseball's ultimate WAR-ior due to his contributions at the plate, on the bases, and in the field. He truly is a fantastic all-around player, excelling at every position he is asked to play.

CHAPTER 3

BRYCE "MONDO" HARPER

On May 9, 2015, nearly forty thousand fans stood as one at Nationals Park. Their hero was up to bat, and he had a chance to win the game.

On that sun-splashed Saturday afternoon, the Washington Nationals and the visiting Atlanta Braves were tied 6–6 in the bottom of the ninth inning. Bryce Harper crouched in the left batter's box. With eye black smeared over his cheekbones, above his iconic beard, Harper seemingly snarled at the pitcher. The Nationals' young star was surging with confidence. Two games earlier, he had socked three home runs against Miami. He followed that up with two more homers on Friday. Would he now belt his sixth home run in three games, this time for a walk-off winner?

Upper-cutting a low breaking ball, Harper launched a rocket. As the ball crashed into the seats, fans jumped for joy and pumped their fists. At just over twenty years old, Harper was already carving out his place in MLB history.

Harper would continue to build his heroic status all season long. With a swing almost identical to Babe

Ruth's, he rifled line drives all over the field and beyond the fences. His hard-charging speed led to a league-best 118 runs scored alongside his crowd-rousing catches in right field. A passionate performer, he was patient enough to draw 124 walks. In 2015, Harper batted .330 (172 ÷ 521 = .330) with a National League (NL)-high 42 home runs. In NL MVP balloting that year, all thirty voters selected Harper. He thus became the youngest unanimous MVP in major league history. Based on his track record, no one was surprised.

PASSIONATE PHENOM

The son of a Las Vegas, Nevada, steelworker, Harper inherited his father's work ethic. While focusing hard in the classroom, he also played baseball year-round. After four-hour practices at Las Vegas High School, he would "go on a dead sprint to his dad's truck because he's going to go hit for another hour and a half," his coach, Sam Thomas, told Chuck Finder of the *Pittsburgh Post-Gazette*.

The results were astounding. At age twelve, while playing in a tournament with a 250-foot (76-meter) fence, he went 12-for-12 with 11 home runs. At age fifteen, he crushed a 570-foot (174 m) home run. At sixteen, he made the cover of *Sports Illustrated* next to the headline "Baseball's Chosen One."

After two years of high school, Harper enrolled at the College of Southern Nevada. His plan was to earn his GED—the equivalent of a high school diploma—while simultaneously playing college baseball. As a freshman in 2009, while playing catcher, Harper cracked 101 hits in 228 at-bats, good for a batting average of .443 (101 ÷ 228 = .443). He logged thirty-one homers in sixty-six games. In an important postseason game, he had six hits in six at-bats: a double, a triple, and four home runs. His twenty-one total bases for the game included two for the double, three for the triple, and sixteen for the four home runs. Though he was just sixteen years old, Harper

Playing for Las Vegas High School in 2008–2009, Harper batted .569 with thirty-seven hits in sixty-five at-bats; he also stole twenty-one bases.

won the Golden Spikes Award as the top amateur player in the country.

In 2010, the Nationals drafted Bryce first overall. His uniform number, 34, is actually based on a math equation. His favorite player was legendary New York Yankee Mickey Mantle, who wore number 7. Thus, adding the numerals of Harper's 34 produced the iconic 7 worn by Mantle.

When he debuted in the majors on April 27, 2012, Harper was just nineteen years old. A highly aggressive player, he exhibited a fiery intensity at the plate and on the bases. After Phillies pitcher Cole Hamels hit him with a pitch on May 6, Bryce made him pay. He moved to third base and stole home, sticking it to the pitcher.

Five days later, Harper proved to be a little overly aggressive. Out of anger, he smashed his bat against the dugout wall—and the bat bounced off the wall and hit him above the eye. Blood flowed, and he needed stitches to close the wound.

Harper made the NL All-Star team as a rookie, becoming the youngest position player ever to participate in the MLB All-Star Game. As a rookie, he batted .270 ($144 \div 533 = .270$) with twenty-two homers and eighteen stolen bases. Teammates praised him for his work ethic, exuberance, and just being one of the guys. At year's end, he and Mike Trout were named NL and AL Rookie of the Year, respectively. Despite receiving the prestigious

HOMETOWN DERBY

Harper never won a playoff series with Washington, but he was crowned a champion on a magical summer night in 2018.

In front of an electric, sellout crowd at Nationals Park, Harper participated in MLB's annual Home Run Derby, which takes place the night before the All-Star Game. With red, white, and blue on his bat, headband, batting gloves, and armband, he lit up the sky with his rocketing home runs. With his dad serving as his pitcher—just like during his childhood days in Las Vegas—Harper reached the finals. That is where the real fireworks began.

Kyle Schwarber batted first in the final round and launched eighteen balls over the fence. Harper, stuck on nine homers with less than a minute left, seemed doomed to defeat. With the crowd supporting him and fire in his belly, however, he went on a longball tear. Like a scene out of a movie, he swatted nine home runs in the final fifty seconds to tie Schwarber at eighteen—including the last one as time expired.

In his thirty seconds of bonus time, he skied a towering homer to center field. Harper tossed his bat and hugged his dad as the crowd went wild.

award, Harper said after the season his most important goal was not individual achievement—but to bring a World Series title to the city of Washington, DC.

NATIONAL TREASURE

The Nationals, who have only been in the majors since 2005, finally had a superstar—but he had trouble staying healthy. Overly aggressive, Harper ran into an outfield wall in 2013, hurting his knee. In 2014, he injured his thumb on a slide. Not until 2015 did he play a full season again—and what a year it was. Harper led the NL in on-base percentage (.460), slugging average (.649), and OPS (1.109). OPS stands for on-base percentage plus slugging average, so its calculation is a simple addition of those two statistics:

OBP: (172 + 124 + 5) ÷ (521 + 124 + 5 + 4) = .460
Slugging average: ((91) + (38 × 2) + (1 × 3) + (42 × 4)) ÷ 521 = .649
OPS: .460 + .649 = 1.109

In recent years, baseball's best hitters are often measured by OPS. The reason for that is simple: if a player gets on base a lot (high OBP) and slugs a lot of singles, doubles, triples, and homers, he is certainly a productive offensive player. Looking at either of those statistics individually may not paint a clear picture of what that player brings to the team, but OPS accurately reflects both factors.

In his seven seasons up to 2018, Harper made the NL All-Star team six times. He batted .319 (134 ÷ 420 = .319) in 2017 and led the majors with 130 walks in 2018.

Fans across the nation have appreciated his patriotism as well as his play. In multiple Fourth of July games, he has worn red, white, and blue and stars and stripes on his bat, cleats, and batting gloves. On July 4, 2015, he belted a home run with his star-spangled bat, electrifying Nationals Park in the process.

Harper is driven to improve, excel, and win. That hard-charging attitude propelled him to the MLB All-Star Game as a nineteen-year-old rookie.

Prior to Harper, the Nationals had never had a winning season. With him—along with other stars such as pitchers Stephen Strasburg and Max Scherzer—they won four NL East Division titles from 2012 through 2017. In 2017, they won the division by a huge margin. Washington went 97–65, and the second-place Miami Marlins finished 77–85.

In MLB division standings, one important stat is games behind (GB). To calculate how many games back one

In February 2019, Harper signed with the Philadelphia Phillies. He was guaranteed $330 million over thirteen years, making it the largest player contract in baseball history.

team is from another, subtract the worse team's number of wins from the better team's; then, subtract the better team's number of losses from the worse team's; add both of those numbers up and divide by two to produce GB. For example, the second-place Marlins were twenty games back from the Nationals in 2017:

$$97 - 77 = 20$$
$$85 - 65 = 20$$
$$20 + 20 = 40$$

$40 \div 2 = 20$

Unfortunately for Nationals fans, the team still did not win a playoff series through 2018. In four NL Division Series, Harper and his mates lost all four—three of them in close heartbreakers. Thus, Harper unfortunately never came close to his dream of bringing a World Series title to Washington. After the 2018 season, he signed as a free agent with the Philadelphia Phillies.

CHAPTER 4

MARKUS "MOOKIE" BETTS

When it comes to home runs, Mookie Betts both hits them and takes them away. Baltimore Orioles manager Buck Showalter—who has been in professional baseball for more than four decades—has described Mookie as the best defensive right fielder he has ever seen. On September 25, 2015, Showalter witnessed Betts at his best.

That night at Boston's Fenway Park, the Red Sox led Baltimore 7–0 with two outs in the top of the ninth inning. Pitcher Rich Hill was one out away from his first shutout in nine years. For several seconds, the shutout seemed on the verge of disappearing. Orioles slugger Chris Davis crushed a pitch deep to right field.

That is when Betts came to his pitcher's rescue. The speedy right fielder raced toward the fence and leaped as high as he could. As he did, his hip collided with the top of the fence and his body tipped over the barrier like a teeter-totter. As Mookie's head dipped into the bullpen, the ball landed in his glove. Slowly, he teetered his body upward and back into the field of play—revealing the ball in his mitt. He prevented the home run and helped his pitcher out in a single jump and catch combination.

BASEBALL, BASKETBALL, AND BOWLING

Markus "Mookie" Betts, just twenty-six years old in 2019, is a true five-tool talent: power, speed, high batting average, great defense, and a strong arm.

Betts always runs direct routes to the ball and stretches out to make grabs, like in this leaping catch against the Angels in 2016.

Though standing just 5 feet 9 inches (175 cm) tall, Betts is wiry strong. He has twice belted thirty home runs in a season, and he has hammered three home runs in an MLB game four times; Babe Ruth achieved that feat only three times across his entire storied career. On the bases, Betts is a dangerous weapon. He has stolen 110 bases (through 2018) in 132 attempts. That is a success rate of 83 percent, which can be calculated by dividing the number of successful steals by the number of attempted steals:

110 ÷ 132 = .83 (83 percent)

Because the result is a percentage, move the decimal point two places to the right. In 2018, MLB players overall stole bases at just a 72 percent success rate.

As for pure hitting, Betts led the majors with a .346 batting average in 2018 (180 ÷ 520 = .346). In right field, he won the AL Gold Glove Award in 2016, 2017, and 2018. Betts was the only player in the American League to win three Gold Gloves from 2016 through 2018; he is simply that good. He also packs a laser beam for an arm. On June 16, 2017, Houston's George Springer tried to score from second base on a single to right field. Betts fielded the ball on one hop and fired a strike to the catcher. Statcast measured the speed of his throw at a blistering 96.8 mph (155.8 kph).

Outside of baseball, Betts also starred in basketball in high school, and he was capable of dunking despite his small size. In college, he shined defensively at second base. He even once recorded a perfect 300 score during a professional bowling event. Though his basketball and bowling skills do not play a direct part in his on-field baseball success, they speak to a more important factor in Betts's game: sheer versatility.

Growing up outside Nashville, Tennessee, Betts was not content with just learning to walk. "He never walked," Mookie's father, Willie Betts, told Jen McCaffrey of MassLive.com. "If you put him down, he'd start running. He would just run, run, run." While he was running, rattles and squeaky toys were not his objects of desire. "He'd always be saying, 'Ball? Ball? Ball?' That's what he always wanted to do," his mother, Diana Benedict, told McCaffrey.

Betts would become masterful at many ball sports. Playing basketball at Overton High School in Nashville, he was named league MVP as a senior after averaging fourteen points and nine assists per game. As a junior, he batted .548 in baseball and was named Tennessee boys Bowler of the Year.

In 2011, the Red Sox drafted Betts right out of high school. In 2013, he emerged as a hot minor league prospect. In 2014, he batted .355 (76 ÷ 214 = .355) for Portland and .335 (62 ÷ 185 = .335) for Pawtucket. By adding his raw hits and at-bats statistics, it is possible to calculate his overall batting average in the minors in 2014. Betts had 76 hits in 214 at-bats for Portland, and 62 hits in 185 at-bats for Pawtucket. So, 76 + 62 = 138 total hits; 214 + 185 = 399 total at-bats; 138 hits ÷ 399 at-bats = .346 overall minor league average in 2014.

Even in the minor leagues, Betts's skill was obvious; with terrific swing mechanics and lightning-fast reflexes, he rocketed balls deep into the seats.

BETTS ... AS IN BEST

Betts played fifty-two games for the Red Sox in 2014, batting .291 (55 ÷ 189 = .291). Though this average was not bad, it was not until the next season that he began to flash his star power. On Opening Day in Boston, he belted a home run, stole two bases, and robbed Bryce Harper of a home run—all in the first three innings. He finished the season with a .291 (174 ÷ 597 = .291) average, forty-two doubles, eighteen homers, and twenty-one steals.

Known for his relentless work ethic, Betts took his game to a higher level in 2016. He batted .318 (214 ÷ 672 = .318) with 42 doubles, 31 homers, 26 steals, 122 runs scored, and 113 RBI. As amazing as he was offensively, he created even more magic in right field. He led AL right fielders in putouts (meaning catches) with 346. He finished second among league right fielders with fourteen assists, meaning throwing guys out on the bases, and he led all AL outfielders with a .997 fielding percentage.

The formula for fielding percentage is (putouts + assists) ÷ (putouts + assists + errors). Betts committed just one error on the year, so:

(346 + 14) ÷ (346 + 14 + 1)
360 ÷ 361 = .997

When batters get two strikes, they often strike out or make weak contact on the next pitch. Betts batted .300 when he had two strikes in 2018.

Throughout 2016, Mookie made numerous running, sliding, diving, twisting, and leaping grabs. Statisticians calculated that his defensive work saved thirty-two runs. No other right fielder in the majors had more than twenty-two runs saved. Betts made such an impact on offense and defense that he finished runner-up to Mike Trout for AL MVP.

Mookie's numbers dipped in 2017 to a .264 batting average (166 ÷ 628 = .264), 26 homers, 101 runs, and 102 RBI. In 2018, however, he roared to the AL MVP Award with his best season yet. The AL batting champion at .346 (180 ÷ 520 = .346), he amassed 47 doubles, 32 homers, and 30 stolen bases. He paced ALers in both runs scored (129) and slugging percentage (.640): his 333 total bases (96 singles, 47 doubles, 5 triples, 32 homers) ÷ 520 at-bats = .640.

Although Betts batted just .210 (13 ÷ 62 = .210) in the 2018 postseason, the talent-loaded Red Sox

LOVABLE MONSTER

For more than a century, Red Sox fans have savored the charms of Fenway Park. Lushly green—both the grass and the walls—Fenway features quirky fencing. The Green Monster wall towers 37 feet (11.2 m) in left field, but is only 310 feet (94.5 m) from home plate. The right field fence goes up to Mookie Betts's chest, but it is a full 380 feet (115.8 m) from the plate at its deepest point.

In general, right-handed batters tend to pull the ball to left field. Thus, right-handed hitters love Fenway, often banging balls off or over the Green Monster. In 2018, Betts batted .364 (86 ÷ 236 = .364) at home.

Along with Babe Ruth, Ted Williams has often been called the greatest hitter of the twentieth century. The Splendid Splinter played nineteen seasons with Boston. However, he missed more than 700 games—during the prime years of his career—due to military service in World War II and the Korean War. Yet he still batted .344 (2,654 ÷ 7,706 = .344) for his career with 521 home runs.

Ironically, Williams was a left-handed pull hitter, so Fenway's dimensions actually hurt his home run numbers. He swatted more home runs on the road (273) than at home (248), though he batted a stellar .361 (1,403 ÷ 3,887 = .361) at home for his career.

Betts poses with the 2018 American League MVP Award. He sparked the Red Sox to 108 wins that year, the most in team history.

cruised to the World Series title. In fact, Betts became the first player in major league history to achieve the following accolades in the same season: batting title, MVP Award, Gold Glove Award, Silver Slugger Award (as the best hitter at his position), and World Series title. His regular-season WAR was 10.9—the highest by any MLB player since Barry Bonds in 2002.

"I've played with some great players," veteran Red Sox second baseman Dustin Pedroia told Alex Speier of the *Boston Globe*. "I don't think I've seen a season with an all-around game like that. He's always been elite, but he's gone to another level."

Betts entered 2019 at the tender age of twenty-six, with fans expecting a whole lot more Mookie magic in the years to come.

CHAPTER 5

WHO IS THE GOAT?

GOAT was not a term used in 1920. Nevertheless, many fans that year were calling Babe Ruth the greatest player of all time. How could they not? Ruth was the first star pitcher who could also hit well at the major league level—and not just well. In 1920, he put up the biggest offensive numbers in major league history at the time.

A century later, most fans still call Ruth the best of all time—but is he really? Is he superior to old-school greats Ty Cobb, Ted Williams, or Barry Bonds—let alone modern superstars Mike Trout, Bryce Harper, and Mookie Betts—or is he coasting on his own legendary status? For one thing, it is difficult to compare players across eras, as the game changes a lot over time. For that reason, it is worth investigating the best player of the twentieth century and the best player of the twenty-first century, then comparing their statistics.

Admirers of Ruth gifted him this crown, signifying his king-like status in baseball. He still remains the game's biggest legend.

GO20C: GREATEST OF THE 20TH CENTURY

As the 1900s concluded, the *Sporting News* named Ruth the greatest baseball player of all time. *Sports Illustrated* has also proclaimed Ruth—with his .342 career average and 714 home runs—the best player in MLB history.

Other legends have also laid claim to the MLB's top dog title over the years. Ty Cobb, the fiery Detroit Tiger from the early 1900s, owns the highest batting average of all time: .366 (4,189 ÷ 11,439). Though he cracked only 117 career home runs, he stole 897 bases.

From 1927 to 1937, Yankees legend Lou Gehrig batted .350 (2,222 ÷ 6,350 = .350) with 39 homers and

154 RBI per season. Amyotrophic lateral sclerosis (Lou Gehrig's disease, or ALS) cut short his career. He finished with a .340 (2,721 ÷ 8,001 = .340) career average and 493 homers.

Willie Mays was the Mike Trout of the mid-1900s—a versatile and talented center fielder. He amassed 660 homers and 338 steals, though batted only .302 (3,283 ÷ 10,881). Ted Williams's offensive numbers were similar to Ruth's, with a .344 (2,654 ÷ 7,706 = .344) average and 521 home runs. He ranks first all-time in OBP at .482 (Ruth is second) and second to Ruth in slugging and OPS.

"Hammerin'" Hank Aaron broke Ruth's home run record with 755, and his 2,297 RBI are still tops all-time. However, his career batting average was only .305 (3,771 ÷ 12,364 = .305). Pittsburgh and San Francisco slugger Barry Bonds played from 1986 to 2007. He holds the MLB career home run record with 762, but he batted just .298 (2,935 ÷ 9,847 = .298). He has not been elected to the Baseball Hall of Fame because he was credibly accused of using performance-enhancing drugs.

WAR, the complex stat that measures a player's overall value to his teams, favors the Babe in a competition between twentieth-century greats. His career WAR (182.5) is by far the highest of all time. Among position players, Bonds is next at 162.8, followed by Mays (156.4), Cobb (151.1), and Aaron (143.0).

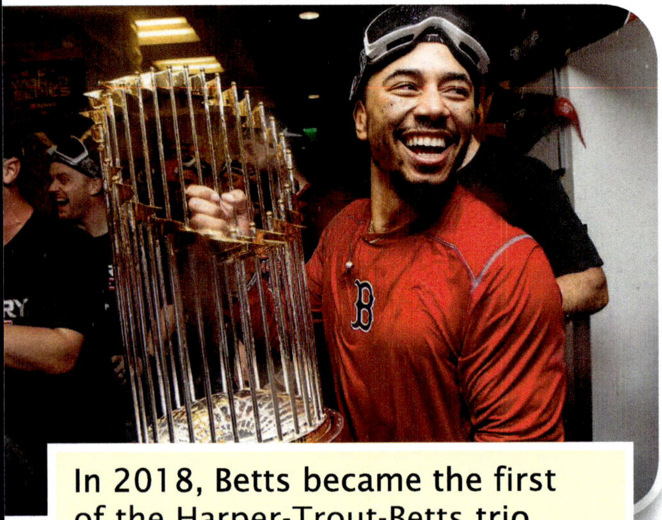

In 2018, Betts became the first of the Harper-Trout-Betts trio to win a World Series—though he was helped by a loaded Red Sox roster.

Moreover, the Great Bambino revolutionized the game with his home runs while still batting .342 and blowing away hitters with his pitching. It is no wonder that the Associated Press named Ruth not just the greatest baseball player, but the top athlete overall of the twentieth century.

GO21C: Greatest of the 21st Century

In terms of stats and accomplishments, it is easy to compare Trout, Harper, and Betts. They are all outfielders, they play in the same era, and they are each about the same age. Trout was born in 1991, while Bryce and Mookie were born in 1992.

Below is a list of their career stats and honors through 2018. Use your analytic reasoning to determine who you think is the best of the three.

Player	Trout	Harper	Betts
Games	1,065	927	644
WAR	64.3	27.4	35.2
Batting AVG	.307	.279	.303
Home Runs	240	184	110
Steals	189	75	110
Runs	793	610	478
RBI	648	521	390
OBP	.416	.388	.370
SLG	.573	.512	.518
OPS	.990	.900	.888
All-Star Games	7	6	3
MVP Awards	2	1	1
MVP Top 5	7	1	2
Gold Gloves	0	0	3
World Series Titles	0	0	1
Made Playoffs	1	4	3

Of the three, Trout seems to have the best stats. However, Betts is the only one with Gold Gloves and a World Series title. Harper has led his team to the postseason the most often, largely because of his leadership, though he has not yet captured a championship. Harper, who has battled injuries, was the unanimous NL MVP in 2015, and his potential for more greatness is tremendous. The latter can be said for all three superstars.

GOAT: GREATEST OF ALL TIME

Statisticians have come up with many complex statistics, such as WAR, to compare players from multiple eras. However, it is still impossible to determine how well players from decades ago would fare today, and vice versa.

Yes, most baseball historians say Ruth is the greatest ever. The reasoning is simple and is easily backed up by raw stats: he dominated the competition of his day more than any other player has ever dominated this sport. He also played during the formative years of the game, before technology, nutrition, and training evolved to the elite form of the twenty-first century. Whether Ruth could have adapted to a healthy lifestyle—with few hot dogs and little alcohol and smoking—had he been born into the modern game is a matter of debate. It is a fact, however, that the competition he faced in the 1920s was nowhere near as strong as the competition and talent today. He smashed his way to success hitting pitches that topped out in the mid–80 mph (128.7 kph) range; today, pitchers sling the ball at closer to 100 mph (160.9 kph).

Some professionals and experts do not believe the Bambino would have been able to make it in modern MLB. His style was powerful and a bit wild—but today's game is largely about discipline and attention to detail.

WAR LEADERS

Below is the all-time WAR list, through 2018. Note that Mike Trout has a WAR of 64.3 after just eight seasons. His WAR per season is thus 8.0 (64.3 ÷ 8 seasons = 8.0). If he averaged 8.0 per season for 20 seasons, his WAR would read 160 (8.0 × 20 = 160).

RANK	PLAYER	CAREER WAR RATING
1	BABE RUTH	182.4
2	WALTER JOHNSON	164.3
3	CY YOUNG	163.6
4	BARRY BONDS	162.8
5	WILLIE MAYS	156.4
6	TY COBB	151.0
7	HANK AARON	143.0
8	ROGER CLEMENS	139.2
9	TRIS SPEAKER	134.0
10	HONUS WAGNER	130.8

Some, however, believe he was naturally talented enough to succeed and adapt.

Ruth once underwent a series of tests to measure his power, reflexes, hand-eye coordination, and more. For example, he had to insert a cylindrical instrument into round holes as frequently as he could in sixty seconds. Amazingly, he registered 122 hits with his right hand, and 132 with his left. "The tests proved that the coordination of eye, brain, nerve system, and muscle is practically perfect," reported Hugh S. Fullerton in *Popular Science* magazine. With this incredible innate physical ability, it is likely Ruth could have made it in modern MLB. Though swinging mechanics and an eye for the ball are indisputably important for a hitter, so, too, are fast reflexes and a quick-twitch response to a pitch. Ruth had basic skills in spades, so it is likely he would have been incredible in the modern game.

However, what if Trout, Harper, and Betts played in the 1920s? Without the advantages of year-round youth programs, modern weight training equipment, dieting advice, video feedback, and modern medicine, they may not have made it into the big leagues to begin with. Could Trout and Betts rob home runs with the old pancake gloves of old? Like Ruth, all three of these young superstars have raw abilities that transcend time and training, so they would have probably been dominant forces in the twentieth century, as well.

However, these are things that can never be known. To determine baseball's GOAT, all anyone can do is study the statistics, do some math, and look at footage of the old players and those of today. It is also important to read about the differences between eras and listen to experts.

In the end, talking about who is better than whom is a matter of opinion—and is one of the many reasons

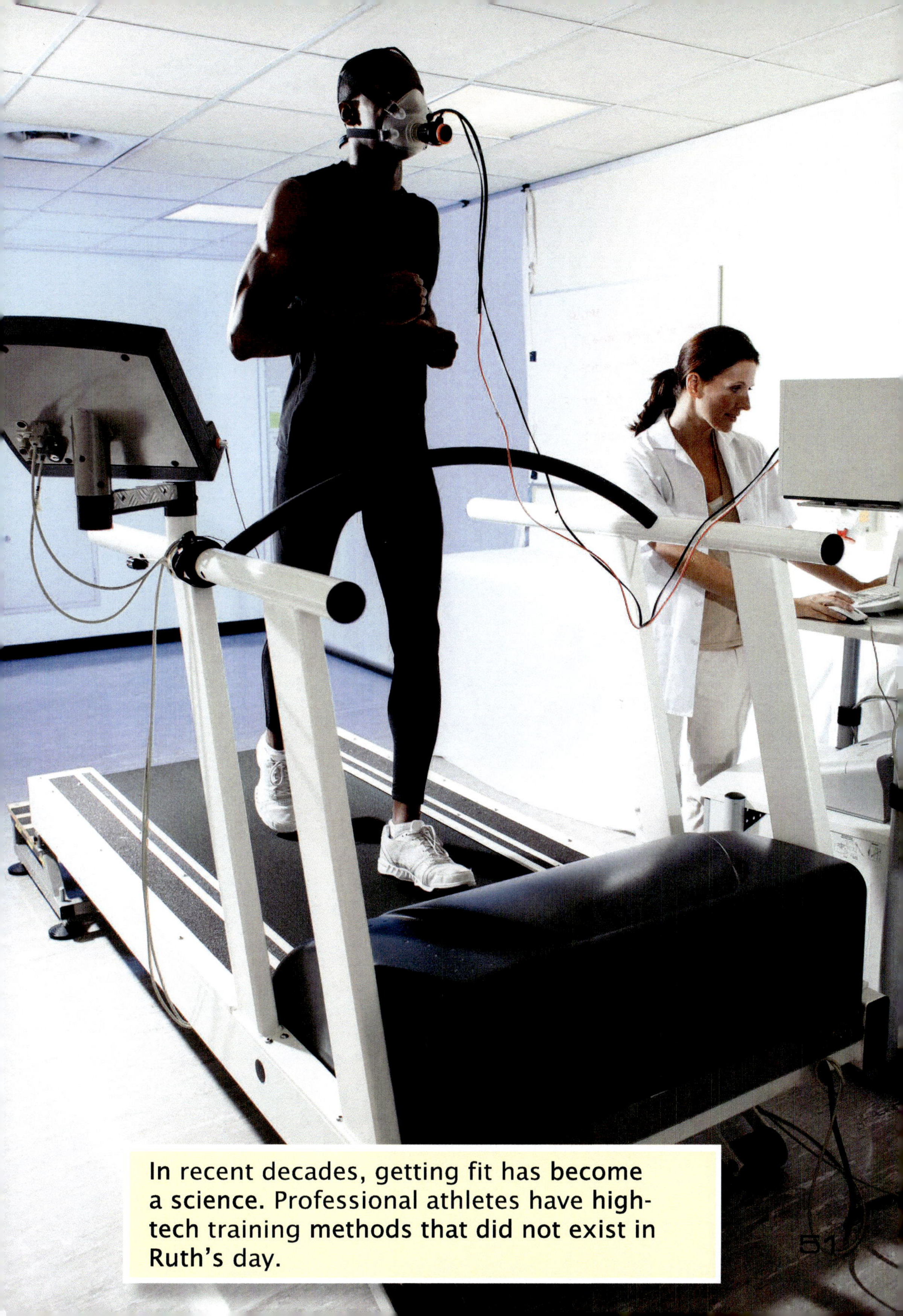

In recent decades, getting fit has become a science. Professional athletes have high-tech training methods that did not exist in Ruth's day.

millions of fans love the game. Ruth was an unstoppable force for a long time—but he also played a long time ago. Trout, Harper, and Betts are impressive players in their own right, but some may argue that recency bias, or a tendency of sports fans to glorify newer or current players, plays a part in considering any of them the GOAT. After all, baseball—like all sports—is constantly evolving and, typically, improving. Decades-old achievements do not look as impressive as modern records. Using math as a tool to compare old and new, the old guard against the new blood, it is possible to come up with some answers—but not all.

GLOSSARY

Associated Press A US-based news organization made up of journalists from all over the world.

dinger Another name for a home run in baseball.

doubleheader Two games played by two teams against each other in one day.

eye black Black grease or a black strip applied under the eyes to reduce glare.

fielded Describing a ball that has been caught or retrieved after being struck by an opposing batter.

Gold Glove Award Presented by Rawlings to the best defensive player at each position in each league (American League and National League).

hand-eye coordination The coordinated control of eye and hand movement; hitters need to be good at this.

idyllic Happy, peaceful, picturesque.

MVP Award Presented to the Most Valuable Player in the AL and NL; voted on by thirty members of the Baseball Writers Association of America.

phenom A young person with extraordinary (phenomenal) talent.

quotient The result of a formula using the division operator.

radar A system for detecting the presence, direction, distance, and speed of moving objects by sending out pulses of high-frequency electromagnetic waves that reflect off the object and come back to the source.

rotunda A large, round room or building.

scout A person who evaluates players and reports back to the team that he or she works for.

shutout A game in which one team does not score.

statistician An expert in the compilation, creation, and analysis of statistics.

telegram A message sent by a telegraph machine and then delivered in printed form.

variable Something that can change.

walk-off A batted ball (or walk or hit-by-pitch) that wins the game in the bottom of the ninth inning or the bottom of an extra inning.

wins above replacement (WAR) This relatively new and complex statistic measures a player's overall value.

FOR MORE INFORMATION

American Mathematical Society (AMS)
201 Charles Street
Providence, RI 02904
Website: https://www.ams.org
Facebook, Instagram, and Twitter: @amermathsoc
The AMS promotes math education. It features resources for students interested in learning more about math and its applications outside the classroom.

Baseball Canada
2212 Gladwin Crescent, Suite A7
Ottawa, ON K1B 5N1
Canada
Website: https://www.baseball.ca
Facebook, Instagram, and Twitter: @baseballcanada
Baseball Canada is the organization that oversees all amateur baseball leagues and programs in Canada. It is a valuable starting point for anyone interested in the sport.

Baseball Reference
6757 Greene Street, Suite 315
Philadelphia, PA 19119
Website: https://www.baseball-reference.com
Twitter: @baseball_ref
Baseball Reference provides complete statistics on every current and former MLB player and team, including complex stats such as WAR and range factor, among many others.

Canadian Baseball Network
28 Ted Rogers Way
Toronto, ON M4Y 2J4
Canada
Website: https://www.canadianbaseballnetwork.com
Facebook: @canadianbaseballnetwork
Instagram and Twitter: @CDNBaseball
This site features exhaustive information on Canadians formerly, currently, or prospectively playing in MLB.

Entertainment and Sports Programming Network (ESPN)
ESPN Plaza
Bristol, CT 06010
Website: http://www.espn.com
Facebook, Instagram, and Twitter: @ESPN
ESPN is one of the premiere sports news organizations in the world. Its site includes news, videos, and stats on all MLB players. ESPN prides itself on independent, objective reporting, whereas official sources largely try to maintain a good reputation for players and the league.

Little League Baseball and Softball
539 US Route 15
Williamsport, PA 17701
Website: https://www.littleleague.org
Facebook, Instagram, and Twitter: @littleleague
Millions of girls and boys worldwide play Little League baseball. This site helps parents and players determine where to sign up and also explains all the official rules of Little League, which are slightly different from MLB rules.

Major League Baseball (MLB)
245 Park Avenue
New York, NY 10167
Website: http://www.MLB.com
Facebook, Instagram, and Twitter: @MLB
The MLB's website features in-depth information on all of its current players, including news stories, highlight videos, stats, and biographical info.

FOR FURTHER READING

Aretha, David. *Top 10 Pitchers in Baseball*. New York, NY: Enslow, 2016.

Christopher, Matt. *Babe Ruth*. Boston, MA: Little, Brown & Co., 2015.

Gitlin, Marty. *Mike Trout: Baseball MVP*. New York, NY: Rosen Publishing, 2018.

Graubert, Norman. *The Science of Baseball*. New York, NY: Rosen Publishing, 2016.

Kramer, S. A. *Baseball's Greatest Hitters: From Ty Cobb to Miguel Cabrera*. New York, NY: Random House, 2015.

Mooney, Carla. *Using Math in Sports*. New York, NY: Rosen Publishing, 2018.

Morey, Allan. *Fantasy Baseball Math: Using Stats to Score Big in Your League*. Mankato, MN: Capstone Publishers, 2017.

Payment, Simone. *Bryce Harper*. New York, NY: Rosen Publishing, 2018.

BIBLIOGRAPHY

Baseball Reference. Various articles. Retrieved March 30, 2019. https://www.baseball-reference.com.

DiGiovanna, Mike. "Angels' Mike Trout Named American League Rookie of the Year." *Los Angeles Times*, November 13, 2012. https://www.latimes.com/sports/la-xpm-2012-nov-13-la-sp-1113-mike-trout-rookie-20121113-story.html.

Dybas, Todd. "Words That Shaped a Middling Season for the Nationals." NBC Sports, December 25, 2018. https://www.nbcsports.com/washington/nationals/words-shaped-middling-season-nationals.

Evans, Bill. "Mike Trout Named American League Rookie of the Year." *South Jersey Times*, November 12, 2012. https://www.nj.com/south-jersey-sports/index.ssf/2012/11/mike_trout_named_american_leag.html.

Frank, Vincent. "MLB Pitcher Has Curious Take on Babe Ruth if He Played Today." Yardbarker, December 11, 2018. https://www.yardbarker.com/mlb/articles/mlb_pitcher_has_curious_take_on_babe_ruth_if_he_played_today/s1_12680_27982859.

Fullerton, Hugh S. "Why Babe Ruth Is the Greatest Home-Run Hitter." *Popular Science*, October 23, 2006. https://www.popsci.com/scitech/article/2006-10/archive-why-babe-ruth-greatest-home-run-hitter.

Hoppes, Lynn. "Offbeat Questions with Angels' Mike Trout." ESPN.com, April 10, 2013. http://www.espn.com/blog/playbook/trending/post/_/id/16034/off-beat-questions-with-angels-mike-trout.

Kilgore, Adam. "Bryce Harper Introduced at Pregame News Conference." *Washington Post*, August 26, 2010. http://voices.washingtonpost.com/nationalsjournal/2010/08/bryce_harper_introduced_at_pre.html.

McCaffrey, Jen. "The Story of Mookie Betts' Rise from Nashville to Boston Red Sox Franchise Cornerstone." MassLive.com, July 15, 2015. https://www.masslive.com/redsox/index.ssf/2015/07/boston_red_sox_mookie_betts.html.

MLB.TV. "Betts' Outstanding Catch." MLB.com, September 25, 2015. https://www.mlb.com/video/betts-outstanding-catch/c-501526283.

MLB.TV. "Harper's Walk-Off Homer." MLB.com, May 9, 2015. https://www.mlb.com/video/harpers-walk-off-homer/c-108309983.

Speier, Alex. "Mookie Betts Is the American League Most Valuable Player." *Boston Globe*, November 15, 2018. https://www.bostonglobe.com/sports/redsox/2018/11/15/mookie-betts-american-league-most-valuable-player/exVMXfmMenxVhAbYkPxf4N/story.html.

Strang, Katie. "Trout's Greatest Catch: The Art of Robbing a Home Run." ESPN.com, September 10, 2016. http://www.espn.com/mlb/story/_/id/17489202/mike-trout-greatest-catch-art-robbing-home-run.

Thomas, Robert Jr. "Johnny Sylvester, the Inspiration for Babe Ruth Heroics, Is Dead." *New York Times*, January 11, 1990. https://www.nytimes.com/1990/01/11/obituaries/johnny-sylvester-the-inspiration-for-babe-ruth-heroics-is-dead.html.

Verducci, Tom. "The Star That Still Won't Shine." *Sports Illustrated*, July 12, 2018. https://www.si.com/mlb/2018/07/12/mike-trout-los-angeles-angels.

Yates, Clinton. "Mookie Betts Is the Superstar Baseball Needs." The Undefeated, November 15, 2018. https://theundefeated.com/features/boston-red-sox-mookie-betts-is-the-superstar-baseball-needs.

INDEX

ABOUT THE AUTHOR

Growing up in Michigan, David Aretha enjoyed math more than any other subject until he discovered the joys of writing. He has authored and edited dozens of sports books, including a book on Babe Ruth. For middle school readers, he authored biographies on Ichiro Suzuki, Alex Rodriguez, and Jose Altuve. And for Topps trading cards, he wrote thousands of back-of-the-card bios on MLB stars.

PHOTO CREDITS

Cover (top left), p. 42 Alex Trautwig/Major League Baseball/ Getty Images, (top right) Mitchell Layton/Getty Images, (bottom left), p. 46 Billie Weiss/Boston Red Sox/Getty Images, (bottom right), pp. 7, 12, 14, 44 Bettmann/Getty Images; pp. 5, 27 Icon Sportswire/Getty Images; p. 9 George Rinhart/Corbis Historical/Getty Images; p. 17 Stephen Dunn/Getty Images; p. 18 Paul Spinelli/Major League Baseball/Getty Images; p. 20 Sean M. Haffey/Getty Images; p. 22 Library of Congress Prints and Photographs Division; p. 31 The Washington Post/ Getty Images; p. 32 Joe Robbins/Getty Images; p. 35 Jayne Kamin-Oncea/Getty Images; p. 38 Portland Press Herald/Getty Images; p. 40 Denis Poroy/Getty Images; p. 51 Science Photo Library/Brand X Pictures/Getty Images.

Design & Layout: Brian Garvey; Editor: Siyavush Saidian; Photo Researcher: Sherri Jackson